Chemistry revision got you at boiling point?

Edexcel's 9-1 GCSE Chemistry exams can get pretty heated, but this CGP book is a great way to stay cool and composed throughout your revision.

It's packed with thirty quick tests covering every topic you need to know. Each one should only take ten minutes, so you won't need to block out hours of your life in one go. Just tackle them one at a time and you'll get there.

And finally, all the answers are included at the back of the book, so checking your work is a breeze! A cooling breeze, obviously.

CGP — still the best ☺

Our sole aim here at CGP is to produce the highest quality books — carefully written, immaculately presented and dangerously close to being funny.

Then we work our socks off to get them out to you — at the cheapest possible prices.

Published by CGP

Editors:
Alex Billings, Emma Clayton, Paul Jordin, Duncan Lindsay

ISBN: 978 1 78908 079 7

With thanks to Karen Wells and Chris Elliss for the proofreading.
With thanks to Ana Pungartnik for the copyright research.

Clipart from Corel®
Illustrations by: Sandy Gardner Artist, email sandy@sandygardner.co.uk
Printed by W&G Baird Ltd, Antrim.

Based on the classic CGP style created by Richard Parsons.

Text, design, layout and original illustrations © Coordination Group Publications Ltd. (CGP) 2018
All rights reserved.

Photocopying this book is not permitted, even if you have a CLA licence.
Extra copies are available from CGP with next day delivery • 0800 1712 712 • www.cgpbooks.co.uk

Contents

Please note: content from the Key Concepts section is assessable in both Paper 1 and Paper 2.

Key Concepts in Chemistry

Test 1: Key Concepts in Chemistry........................... 2
Test 2: Key Concepts in Chemistry........................... 4
Test 3: Key Concepts in Chemistry........................... 6

Topics for Paper 1

Test 4: States of Matter and Mixtures................... 8
Test 5: States of Matter and Mixtures................. 10
Test 6: Chemical Changes 12
Test 7: Chemical Changes 14
Test 8: Extracting Metals and Equilibria............. 16
Test 9: Extracting Metals and Equilibria............. 18
Test 10: Separate Chemistry 1................................ 20
Test 11: Separate Chemistry 1................................ 22

Mixed Tests for Paper 1

Test 12: Paper 1 Mixed Topics................................ 24
Test 13: Paper 1 Mixed Topics................................ 26
Test 14: Paper 1 Mixed Topics................................ 28
Test 15: Paper 1 Mixed Topics................................ 30
Test 16: Paper 1 Mixed Topics................................ 32

Topics for Paper 2

Test 17: Groups in the Periodic Table................. 34
Test 18: Groups in the Periodic Table................. 36
Test 19: Rates of Reaction
         and Energy Changes............................... 38
Test 20: Rates of Reaction
         and Energy Changes............................... 40
Test 21: Fuels and Earth Science........................... 42
Test 22: Fuels and Earth Science........................... 44
Test 23: Separate Chemistry 2............................... 46
Test 24: Separate Chemistry 2............................... 48
Test 25: Separate Chemistry 2............................... 50

Mixed Tests for Paper 2

Test 26: Paper 2 Mixed Topics................................ 52
Test 27: Paper 2 Mixed Topics................................ 54
Test 28: Paper 2 Mixed Topics................................ 56
Test 29: Paper 2 Mixed Topics................................ 58
Test 30: Paper 2 Mixed Topics................................ 60

Answers 62

Progress Chart... 67

Test 1: Key Concepts in Chemistry

There are **12 questions** in this test. Give yourself **10 minutes** to answer them all.

1. Magnesium has 12 electrons. What will its electronic configuration be?

   A   6.6
   B   8.4
   C   2.8.2
   [1]

2. What type of structure does graphite have?

   A   Giant covalent
   B   Simple molecular
   C   Ionic lattice
   [1]

3. What name is given to the total number of protons and neutrons in an atom?

   A   Isotopic abundance
   B   Atomic number
   C   Mass number
   [1]

4. How are electrons arranged in an atom?

   A   Scattered within a ball of positive charge.
   B   As a cloud within the nucleus.
   C   In shells at fixed distances from the nucleus.
   [1]

5. What type of bond is formed when two hydrogen atoms form a molecule?

   A   An ionic bond
   B   A compound bond
   C   A covalent bond
   [1]

6. True or False? "One mole of oxygen contains more molecules than one mole of hydrogen."

   A   True
   B   False
   [1]

7. Which of the following is a typical physical property of non-metals?

   A   Good conductor of electricity
   B   Shiny
   C   Low boiling point
   [1]

8. In substances containing small molecules...

   A   ...the intermolecular forces are much stronger than the covalent bonds within the molecules.
   B   ...the covalent bonds within the molecules are much stronger than the intermolecular forces.
   C   ...the covalent bonds within the molecules are the same strength as the intermolecular forces.
   [1]

9. In the modern periodic table, what do the electronic configurations of elements in the same group have in common?

....
[1]

10. Balance the following chemical equation:

........Li + ...H_2O → ....LiOH + ...H_2

[1]

11. 66 g of carbon are burnt completely in oxygen to produce CO_2.

The equation for the reaction is: $C + O_2 \rightarrow CO_2$.

Calculate the mass of CO_2 produced.

Relative atomic masses (A_r): C = 12, O = 16

....

....

....

....

.... g
[3]

12. Describe the bonding in an O_2 molecule.

....

....

....
[2]

15

Test 2: Key Concepts in Chemistry

There are **12 questions** in this test. Give yourself **10 minutes** to answer them all.

1. Giant covalent structures have...

   A ...high melting points.

   B ...low melting points.
   [1]

2. Mendeleev used his periodic table to predict the properties of elements that hadn't been discovered at the time.
   He based his predictions on properties of...

   A ...elements in the same row.

   B ...elements in the same column.

   C ...elements with the same atomic mass.
   [1]

3. True or False? "A group is a vertical column in the periodic table."

   A True

   B False
   [1]

4. True or False? "Ionic compounds conduct electricity when dissolved in water but not when molten."

   A True

   B False
   [1]

5. Which of the following features is present in metallic bonding?

   A Delocalised electrons

   B A shared pair of electrons

   C Two oppositely charged ions
   [1]

6. The molecular formula of butanoic acid is $C_4H_8O_2$. What is its empirical formula?

   A C_2H_4O

   B CH_2O

   C CHO
   [1]

7. When calcium is burned in an open container, it reacts with oxygen in the air to form calcium oxide. The reactants in excess is...

   A ...calcium.

   B ...oxygen.

   C ...calcium oxide.
   [1]

8. True or False? "Simple molecular substances are generally good conductors of electricity."

   A True

   B False
   [1]

Key Concepts in Chemistry

9. What are isotopes?

   ....

   ....
   [1]

10. 0.00025 kg of NaOH are dissolved in 0.5 dm³ of water.
    What is the concentration of the solution, in g dm⁻³?

    ....

    ....

    ....

    .... g dm⁻³
    [2]

11. Solid sodium chloride has a giant ionic lattice structure. Describe this structure.

    ....

    ....

    ....
    [2]

12. Explain why graphite can conduct electricity.

    ....

    ....

    ....
    [2]

Test 3: Key Concepts in Chemistry

There are **11 questions** in this test. Give yourself **10 minutes** to answer them all.

1. What is the Avogadro constant?

   A   The number of particles in one mole of substance.

   B   The volume that one mole of gas occupies.

   C   The relative atomic masses of all the atoms in a molecule added together.

   [1]

2. An atom of phosphorus has atomic number 15 and mass number 31. Which of the following statements about this atom is true?

   A   It has 15 protons and 16 electrons.

   B   It has 15 electrons and 16 neutrons.

   C   It has 15 neutrons and 16 protons.

   [1]

3. Why do ionic compounds have high boiling points?

   A   The forces between the ions are weak.

   B   It takes a lot of energy to overcome the forces between the ions.

   [1]

4. How can you calculate the number of moles in a given mass in grams?

   A   Mass ÷ relative formula mass

   B   Relative formula mass ÷ mass

   C   Relative formula mass × mass

   [1]

5. Which of the following explains why solid metals can conduct electricity?

   A   They have a giant structure.

   B   They are held together by strong electrostatic attraction.

   C   They contain delocalised electrons.

   [1]

6. Which of the following is an advantage of using the ball and stick model to represent a molecule?

   A   The gaps between the atoms in the molecule are accurately shown.

   B   The relative sizes of the atoms in the molecule are accurately shown.

   C   The arrangement of all the atoms is shown.

   [1]

7. True or False? "During a chemical reaction no atoms are created or destroyed."

   A   True

   B   False

   [1]

8. What is the relative formula mass (M_r) of KOH? Relative atomic masses (A_r): H = 1, O = 16, K = 39

   A   39

   B   28

   C   56

   [1]

9. Describe how ions are formed when a Group 1 element reacts with a Group 7 element.

....

.... [1]

10. Describe the structure of carbon nanotubes and state the feature of their structure that allows them to conduct electricity.

....

....

....

....

.... [3]

11. Work out the number of molecules in 160 g of the simple molecular compound sulfur dioxide, SO_2.

Avogadro constant = 6.02×10^{23}
Relative atomic masses (A_r): O = 16, S = 32

....

....

....

number of molecules = ... [3]

Topics for Paper 1

Test 4: States of Matter and Mixtures

There are **11 questions** in this test. Give yourself **10 minutes** to answer them all.

1. Which of the following is used to separate mixtures in fractional distillation?

   A Differences in melting point

   B Differences in boiling point

   C Differences in solubility
   [1]

2. In which state of matter are the particles furthest apart?

   A Solid

   B Liquid

   C Gas
   [1]

3. What technique (or techniques) would be best for separating a mixture of salt, water and sand?

   A Evaporation

   B Filtration and crystallisation

   C Chromatography
   [1]

4. True or False? "Air is a chemically pure substance."

   A True

   B False
   [1]

5. Which stage of the water treatment process involves passing water through gravel and sand beds to remove small, solid impurities?

   A Filtration

   B Sedimentation

   C Chlorination
   [1]

6. In paper chromatography...

   A ...the solvent is the stationary phase.

   B ...the solvent is the mobile phase.

   C ...the solvent is the mixture of substances being analysed.
   [1]

7. A liquid turns into a solid. What is this process called?

   A Condensation

   B Sublimation

   C Freezing
   [1]

8. Which of the following processes could be used to make sea water potable?

   A Distillation

   B Filtration

   C Chlorination
   [1]

Topics for Paper 1: States of Matter and Mixtures

9. Describe how the arrangement and motion of particles in a substance change as the substance turns from a liquid into a gas.

   ....

   ....

   ....
   [2]

10. A student is using fractional distillation to separate a mixture of two liquid compounds. Some information about the compounds is shown in the table below.

Compound	Boiling point (°C)
Compound 1	97
Compound 2	65

    The student puts the mixture in a flask, with a fractionating column and condenser attached. They heat the flask, so that the mixture boils.
    The temperature at the top of the fractionating column is 70 °C.
    Describe how fractional distillation separates the two compounds.

    ....

    ....

    ....

    ....

    ....
    [3]

11. Explain how the pattern of spots produced in a paper chromatography experiment can be used to distinguish a pure substance from an impure substance.

    ....

    ....
    [2]

Test 5: States of Matter and Mixtures

There are **12 questions** in this test. Give yourself **10 minutes** to answer them all.

1. True or False? "Paper chromatography can be used to separate out the different elements within a compound."

   A True

   B False

   [1]

2. When a substance changes from a gas into a liquid...

   A ...the particles gain energy and move around faster.

   B ...the particles move further apart.

   C ...the particles lose energy and move closer together.

   [1]

3. When using fractional distillation to separate a mixture of liquids in the lab, which liquid will be collected first?

   A The liquid with the lowest boiling point.

   B The liquid with the highest boiling point.

   C The most abundant liquid.

   [1]

4. How many different phases are used in paper chromatography?

   A 1

   B 2

   C 3

   [1]

5. Which of these changes of state does not take place at the boiling point of a substance?

   A Freezing

   B Condensing

   C Boiling

   [1]

6. True or False? "Water used to dilute a substance for chemical analysis should not contain any dissolved salts."

   A True

   B False

   [1]

7. Which of the following processes can be used to obtain a sample of solid sugar from a water and sugar solution?

   A Filtration

   B Chromatography

   C Crystallisation

   [1]

8. What is meant by a chemically pure substance?

   A A mixture in which all substances are in the same state of matter.

   B A substance that contains only one element or chemical compound.

   C A substance that is clear and transparent.

   [1]

Topics for Paper 1: States of Matter and Mixtures

9. A student carries out paper chromatography on a pure substance. The solvent travelled 4.9 cm up the chromatography paper. The substance left a spot 3.2 cm up the paper. What is the R_f value of the substance? Give your answer to 2 significant figures.

$$R_f = \frac{\text{distance travelled by solute}}{\text{distance travelled by solvent}}$$

....

....

$R_f =$ ....
[2]

10. Look at the table below. Which substance is a gas at 90 °C?

	Melting point (°C)	Boiling point (°C)
Ethanol	−114	78
Water	0	100
Iodine	114	184

....
[1]

11. A student wants to use paper chromatography to determine the number of dyes used in an ink. Describe how the student should set up this experiment.

....

....

....

....
[3]

12. A scientist is testing the melting point of water using a block of ice. They take samples of the ice, and find that the samples they test reach their melting points over a range of temperatures. Suggest why this is.

....
[1]

Test 6: Chemical Changes

There are **12 questions** in this test. Give yourself **10 minutes** to answer them all.

1. What does a pH of 7 indicate?

   A   An acidic solution

   B   An alkaline solution

   C   A neutral solution

   [1]

2. True or False? "An insoluble base will react with an acid."

   A   True

   B   False

   [1]

3. What is an alkali?

   A   A soluble base

   B   A soluble acid

   C   An insoluble base

   [1]

4. In electrolysis, at the cathode, positively charged ions...

   A   ...are oxidised.

   B   ...are reduced.

   C   ...dissolve.

   [1]

5. How does the concentration of hydrogen ions in a solution change as the pH increases from 2 to 3?

   A   It increases by a factor of 10.

   B   It decreases by a factor of 10.

   C   It increases by a factor of 1.5.

   [1]

6. A solution of potassium hydroxide reacts with nitric acid to produce...

   A   ...carbon dioxide and water.

   B   ...a metal oxide and water.

   C   ...a salt and water.

   [1]

7. What are the products in the electrolysis of molten potassium bromide?

   A   Potassium metal and oxygen

   B   Hydrogen gas and bromine gas

   C   Potassium metal and bromine gas

   [1]

8. True or False? "Hydroxide ions make solutions acidic."

   A   True

   B   False

   [1]

Topics for Paper 1: Chemical Changes

9. Name the two substances formed in the electrolysis of sodium chloride solution. Explain your reasoning for each one.

   1. ....

   ....

   2. ....

   ....
   [4]

10. Give the ionic equation for the reaction between hydrogen ions and hydroxide ions when an acid reacts with an alkali. Include state symbols in your answer.

   ....
   [1]

11. Copper sulfate is a soluble salt produced in the reaction between copper oxide and sulfuric acid. Give **one** reason why excess copper oxide is added to the sulfuric acid during the production of copper sulfate.

   ....

   ....
   [1]

12. How can limewater be used to test for carbon dioxide?

   ....

   ....
   [1]

Test 7: Chemical Changes

There are **12 questions** in this test. Give yourself **10 minutes** to answer them all.

1. Which of the following reactions does **not** produce water?
   - **A** Hydrochloric acid with magnesium.
   - **B** Sulfuric acid with magnesium oxide.
   - **C** Nitric acid with magnesium carbonate.

   [1]

2. How can a solid salt be obtained from a salt solution?
   - **A** By adding an indicator.
   - **B** By adding a catalyst.
   - **C** By crystallisation of the salt solution.

   [1]

3. True or False? "The higher the concentration of hydrogen ions in a solution, the lower the pH."
   - **A** True
   - **B** False

   [1]

4. Which of the following is an electrolyte?
   - **A** A molten or dissolved ionic compound.
   - **B** An electric current running through a solution.
   - **C** A positively charged electrode.

   [1]

5. Which of the following compounds is insoluble in water?
   - **A** Potassium chloride
   - **B** Calcium carbonate
   - **C** Sodium sulfate

   [1]

6. What colour is litmus in alkaline solutions?
   - **A** Red
   - **B** Purple
   - **C** Blue

   [1]

7. During electrolysis, anions migrate towards the...
   - **A** ...positively charged electrode.
   - **B** ...negatively charged electrode.

   [1]

8. A weak acid is defined as...
   - **A** ...an acid with a low pH.
   - **B** ...an acid with a low concentration.
   - **C** ...an acid that does not fully ionise in solution.

   [1]

Topics for Paper 1: Chemical Changes

9. Name the two products formed in the reaction between sulfuric acid and zinc oxide.

1. ....

2. ....
[2]

10. A student adds a few drops of methyl orange to some dilute hydrochloric acid.
She then slowly adds calcium oxide powder to the solution, until no more will react.
Describe the colour change that the student will observe in the solution.

....
[1]

11. A solution of copper sulfate is electrolysed using copper electrodes.
Write a half equation for the reaction that occurs at the anode.

....
[1]

12. When calcium chloride solution is added to magnesium sulfate solution,
a precipitate of calcium sulfate is formed.
Describe the next steps required to obtain a pure, dry sample of calcium sulfate.

....

....

....

....
[3]

Topics for Paper 1: Chemical Changes

Test 8: Extracting Metals and Equilibria

There are **11 questions** in this test. Give yourself **10 minutes** to answer them all.

1. Which reaction shows the oxidation of iron?

   A $Zn + FeSO_4 \rightarrow ZnSO_4 + Fe$

   B $4Fe + 3O_2 \rightarrow 2Fe_2O_3$

   C $2Fe_2O_3 + 3C \rightarrow 4Fe + 3CO_2$

   [1]

2. True or False? "All metals are found in the ground as ores."

   A True

   B False

   [1]

3. True or False? "Metals below carbon in the reactivity series can be extracted by reduction using carbon."

   A True

   B False

   [1]

4. The main goal of a life-cycle assessment is to assess...

   A ...the total environmental impact of a product.

   B ...the economic cost of a product.

   C ...how long a product will be in use.

   [1]

5. What effect will decreasing the temperature have on the yield of the exothermic reaction in a reversible reaction?

   A Increase it

   B Decrease it

   C Have no effect

   [1]

6. When a reversible reaction occurs in a sealed reaction vessel, when is dynamic equilibrium reached?

   A When all the reactants are used up.

   B When the amounts of products and reactants are equal.

   C When the rates of the forward and reverse reactions are equal.

   [1]

7. Why are bacterial methods used to extract copper from its ore?

   A They're quicker than electrolysis.

   B They're slower than reduction with carbon.

   C They can be used on low-grade ores.

   [1]

8. True or False? "The Haber process is carried out at a very low temperature."

   A True

   B False

   [1]

Topics for Paper 1: Extracting Metals and Equilibria

9. Name a metal that is extracted from its ore by electrolysis, and explain why it is extracted this way.

   Metal: ....

   Explanation: ....

   ....
   [2]

10. A student added pieces of magnesium and iron to two beakers of hydrochloric acid. She noticed that magnesium reacted faster than iron. Describe what the student saw that led her to this conclusion, and explain why magnesium reacts faster than iron.

    ....

    ....

    ....

    ....

    ....
    [3]

11. The reaction used to produce ammonia is: $N_2 + 3H_2 \rightleftharpoons 2NH_3$

    Suggest a source for each of the two reactants in this reaction.

    ....

    ....

    ....
    [2]

Test 9: Extracting Metals and Equilibria

There are **11 questions** in this test. Give yourself **10 minutes** to answer them all.

1. In a reversible reaction, increasing the concentration of reactants will favour the reaction that forms...

   A ...more product until equilibrium is reached again.

   B ...less product until equilibrium is reached again.
   [1]

2. What is phytoextraction?

   A A process that uses displacement reactions to extract copper.

   B A process that uses bacteria to separate metals from low-grade ores.

   C A process that uses plants to separate metals from low-grade ores.
   [1]

3. Decreasing the pressure of a gaseous reversible reaction at equilibrium will cause the equilibrium to...

   A ...move in the direction where there are fewer molecules of gas.

   B ...move in the endothermic direction.

   C ...move in the direction where there are more molecules of gas.
   [1]

4. The reaction between magnesium and copper(II) sulfate is:

   $Mg + CuSO_4 \rightarrow MgSO_4 + Cu$

   Which metal gains electrons during this reaction?

   A Magnesium

   B Copper
   [1]

5. Which of the following metals is most easily oxidised?

   A Sodium

   B Silver

   C Aluminium
   [1]

6. Which of the following is used as a catalyst in the Haber process?

   A Iron

   B Vanadium pentoxide

   C Aluminium oxide
   [1]

7. Iron is usually extracted from its ores by reduction with carbon rather than by electrolysis. This is because...

   A ...reduction with carbon doesn't produce CO_2.

   B ...iron can't be produced from its ores by electrolysis.

   C ...reduction with carbon is cheaper.
   [1]

8. Two metals, Q and R, are tested for their reactions with water. Metal Q reacted with cold water. Metal R reacted with steam, but not with cold water. Which is the more reactive metal?

   A Metal Q

   B Metal R
   [1]

Topics for Paper 1: Extracting Metals and Equilibria

9. Give **four** stages of a product's life that are examined during a life cycle assessment.

   1. ....

   2. ....

   3. ....

   4. ....
   [4]

10. Suggest **two** ways in which recycling metals is better for the environment than extracting new metals from their ores.

    1. ....

    ....

    2. ....

    ....
    [2]

11. Metal A will displace metal B from an aqueous solution of a salt of metal B. What does this tell you about metal A?

    ....
    [1]

Test 10: Separate Chemistry 1

There are **10 questions** in this test. Give yourself **10 minutes** to answer them all.

1. Corrosion occurs when a metal is...

   A ...oxidised.

   B ...reduced.

   C ...dissolved.

   [1]

2. True or False? "Pure metals can be bent because the layers of atoms can slide over each other."

   A True

   B False

   [1]

3. Which of the following will not reduce the percentage yield of a reaction?

   A Side reactions occurring.

   B Starting with less reactants.

   C A reversible reaction not going to completion.

   [1]

4. Why might iron be electroplated with zinc?

   A Zinc is less reactive than iron so provides a protective coating around the iron.

   B Zinc is more reactive than iron so water and oxygen will react with zinc instead of with the iron.

   C To give the iron a lower density.

   [1]

5. What are the three main essential elements contained in fertilisers?

   A Nitrogen, oxygen, potassium

   B Calcium, phosphorus, oxygen

   C Nitrogen, phosphorus, potassium

   [1]

6. Which equation shows the overall reaction in a hydrogen-oxygen fuel cell?

   A hydrogen + carbon dioxide → water + oxygen

   B hydrogen + oxygen → carbon dioxide

   C hydrogen + oxygen → water

   [1]

7. True or False? "Aluminium alloys have a high density but are resistant to corrosion."

   A True

   B False

   [1]

8. What is the atom economy of a reaction?

   A The percentage of reactants changed into desired products.

   B The amount of money the reaction costs to carry out.

   C The total mass of products formed.

   [1]

Topics for Paper 1: Separate Chemistry 1

9. Why is a high pressure of 200 atmospheres used for the Haber process?
Explain its effect on both yield and the rate at which equilibrium is reached.
The chemical equation for the Haber process is:

$$N_{2(g)} + 3H_{2(g)} \rightleftharpoons 2NH_{3(g)}$$

....

....

....

....

....

[3]

10. A 25.0 cm³ sample of potassium hydroxide (KOH) solution
has a concentration of 0.200 mol dm⁻³.
This sample is completely neutralised by 40.0 cm³ of sulfuric acid (H_2SO_4).

$$2KOH + H_2SO_4 \rightarrow K_2SO_4 + 2H_2O$$

Find the concentration of the sulfuric acid in mol dm⁻³.

....

....

....

....

....

....

.... mol dm⁻³
[4]

Test 11: Separate Chemistry 1

There are **11 questions** in this test. Give yourself **10 minutes** to answer them all.

1. What is electroplating?

   A   Removing the surface of a metal object.

   B   A way of coating an object with a thin layer of metal.

   C   Creating an electric plate.

   [1]

2. True or False? "Steel is an alloy made of iron, oxygen and sulfur."

   A   True

   B   False

   [1]

3. Which of these isn't a raw material used in the Haber process?

   A   Hydrogen

   B   Nitrogen

   C   Oxygen

   [1]

4. True or False? "Percentage yield is calculated by dividing the maximum theoretical mass of product by the mass of product actually made and multiplying by 100."

   A   True

   B   False

   [1]

5. Ammonia reacts with nitric acid to produce ammonium nitrate. What is ammonium nitrate used as?

   A   A fertiliser

   B   A catalyst

   C   A base

   [1]

6. Which two things are needed for iron to rust?

   A   Carbon dioxide and hydrogen

   B   Carbon dioxide and water

   C   Oxygen and water

   [1]

7. In a reversible reaction, what effect does a catalyst have on the rate at which equilibrium is reached?

   A   The rate is increased.

   B   The rate is decreased.

   C   It has no effect on the rate.

   [1]

8. Which of the following is not a typical property of transition metals?

   A   High melting point

   B   Low density

   C   Formation of coloured compounds

   [1]

Topics for Paper 1: Separate Chemistry 1

9. A scientist wanted to use the following reaction to produce $MgCl_2$.
   Calculate the atom economy of the reaction.

   $$Mg + 2HCl \rightarrow MgCl_2 + H_2$$

   Relative atomic masses (A_r): H = 1, Mg = 24, Cl = 35.5

   ....

   ....

   .... [2]

10. Zinc can be added to pure copper to form an alloy.
    This alloy can be used to make locking mechanisms for doors.
    Name the alloy. Explain why it is suited for this purpose.

    Alloy: ....

    Explanation: ....

    .... [2]

11. What mass, in g, of carbon dioxide is formed when 120 dm³ of oxygen
    reacts with methane at room temperature and pressure (RTP)?
    The relative formula mass of CO_2 is 44. The molar volume of a gas at RTP is 24 dm³.

    $$CH_{4\,(g)} + 2O_{2\,(g)} \rightarrow CO_{2\,(g)} + 2H_2O_{(g)}$$

    ....

    ....

    ....

    ....

    .... g

    [3]

    15

Mixed Tests for Paper 1

Test 12: Paper 1 Mixed Topics

There are **11 questions** in this test. Give yourself **10 minutes** to answer them all.

1. True or False? "Isotopes of the same element all have the same mass number."

   A   True

   B   False

   [1]

2. In the following example, what physical state is the hydrochloric acid in?
   $Mg_{(s)} + 2HCl_{(aq)} \rightarrow MgCl_{2\,(aq)} + H_{2\,(g)}$

   A   Solid

   B   Gas

   C   Aqueous solution

   [1]

3. Which of the following reactions will produce a precipitate?

   A   Magnesium and sulfuric acid

   B   Sodium carbonate and hydrochloric acid

   C   Lead nitrate and sodium chloride

   [1]

4. Evaporation is an example of a...

   A   ...chemical change.

   B   ...physical change.

   [1]

5. True or False? "Hydrogen is oxidised during the reaction in a hydrogen-oxygen fuel cell."

   A   True

   B   False

   [1]

6. When a metal reacts completely to form a metal oxide, the mass of the metal oxide formed will be...

   A   ...greater than the mass of the metal used.

   B   ...less than the mass of the metal used.

   C   ...the same as the mass of the metal used.

   [1]

7. What is the mass of one mole of $^{12}_{6}C$?

   A   18 g

   B   6 g

   C   12 g

   [1]

8. Which of the following is **not** a method used to extract metals from their ores?

   A   Reduction of ores by carbon

   B   Oxidation of ores by carbon

   C   Electrolysis

   [1]

9. Nitric acid is a strong acid. Explain what this means in terms of ionisation.

....

....
[1]

10. Give **two** typical properties of transition metals that are not usually exhibited by Group 1 or Group 2 metals.

1. ....

2. ....
[2]

11. Ammonium sulfate can be prepared in a laboratory from ammonia and dilute sulfuric acid, using titration and crystallisation methods. Alternatively it can be prepared by industrial methods.

Give **two** differences between the laboratory preparation of ammonium sulfate and the industrial production of ammonium sulfate. Suggest a reason for each difference.

1. ....

....

....

2. ....

....

....
[4]

Test 13: Paper 1 Mixed Topics

There are **12 questions** in this test. Give yourself **10 minutes** to answer them all.

1. Iron has an atomic number of 26. How many electrons does an Fe^{3+} ion have?

   A 23

   B 26

   C 29

   [1]

2. True or False? "The nitrogen used in the Haber process is obtained from air."

   A True

   B False

   [1]

3. True or false? "Reactions with high atom economies produce lots of waste."

   A True

   B False

   [1]

4. What pressure is used in the Haber process?

   A 2 atmospheres

   B 20 atmospheres

   C 200 atmospheres

   [1]

5. Which gas is produced when a metal carbonate reacts with dilute acid?

   A Carbon dioxide

   B Hydrogen

   C Oxygen

   [1]

6. Which of the following **cannot** be used to show that a sample of a solid, soluble dye is impure?

   A Melting point data

   B Paper chromatography

   C Sedimentation

   [1]

7. What is the atomic number of an element?

   A The number of protons in an atom of that element.

   B The number of neutrons in an atom of that element.

   C The total number of protons and neutrons in an atom of that element.

   [1]

8. An ionic compound is made up of Na^+ ions and Br^- ions. What is its formula?

   A NaBr

   B Na_2Br

   C $NaBr_2$

   [1]

Mixed Tests for Paper 1

9. Give **two** advantages of using hydrogen-oxygen fuel cells instead of conventional car engines to power cars.

   1. ....

   2. ....
   [2]

10. The equation below shows a reversible reaction, where A, B, C and D are different gases.

    $$2A + B \rightleftharpoons C + D$$

    Would the forwards or backwards reaction be favoured if the pressure were increased? Explain your answer.

    ....

    ....

    ....
    [2]

11. Some copper chloride solution was electrolysed using inert electrodes. Identify the product that is formed at the cathode. Explain your answer.

    Product: ....

    Explanation: ....

    ....
    [2]

12. Soluble salts can be prepared from an acid and an alkali.
    A student prepares a soluble salt.
    Why shouldn't the student add an excess of alkali to the acid?

    ....

    ....
    [1]

15

Test 14: Paper 1 Mixed Topics

There are **11 questions** in this test. Give yourself **10 minutes** to answer them all.

1. Which of the following best describes the structure of diamond?

   A   Sheets of carbon atoms arranged in hexagons

   B   Rigid giant covalent structure

   C   Giant ionic lattice

   [1]

2. Iron reacts with oxygen to form iron oxide. In this reaction, iron is...

   A   ...oxidised.

   B   ...reduced.

   C   ...neutralised.

   [1]

3. In paper chromatography, what is an R_f value?

   A   The distance travelled by the solvent, measured from the baseline.

   B   The amount of solute that has travelled above the baseline.

   C   The ratio between the distance travelled by the solute and the solvent.

   [1]

4. For a given substance, in which state do the particles have the most energy?

   A   Solid

   B   Liquid

   C   Gas

   [1]

5. An acid with a large number of acid molecules compared to the volume of water is said to be...

   A   ...strong.

   B   ...dilute.

   C   ...concentrated.

   [1]

6. Beryllium is in Group 2 of the periodic table. What is the charge on a beryllium ion in an ionic compound?

   A   2+

   B   1+

   C   2−

   [1]

7. In the following chemical equation, what number should come before HCl to balance the equation?
   $Zn + HCl \rightarrow ZnCl_2 + H_2$

   A   1

   B   2

   C   3

   [1]

8. Which of the following statements about the nucleus of an atom is true?

   A   The nucleus has no charge.

   B   Most of the mass of an atom is found in the nucleus.

   C   The nucleus is very large compared to the overall size of the atom.

   [1]

9. Potassium reacts with water in a vigorous reaction. Copper does not react with water. Explain which metal, potassium or copper, forms cations more easily.

....

....

....
[2]

10. A sodium hydroxide (NaOH) solution has a concentration of 0.5 mol dm^{-3}. What is its concentration in g dm^{-3}?

Relative atomic masses (A_r): H = 1, O = 16, Na = 23

....

....

....

.... g dm^{-3}
[2]

11. A student has a mixture of magnesium sulfate and copper filings. Magnesium sulfate is a solid that is soluble in water. Outline a method the student could use to obtain a pure sample of the magnesium sulfate.

....

....

....

....
[3]

Test 15: Paper 1 Mixed Topics

There are **11 questions** in this test. Give yourself **10 minutes** to answer them all.

1. Which of the following would you expect to have the lowest boiling point?

   A   A giant ionic structure

   B   A simple molecular structure

   C   A giant covalent structure

   [1]

2. Oxidation is...

   A   ...gain of electrons.

   B   ...loss of electrons.

   [1]

3. Which of the processes below is a biological method for extracting metals from their ores?

   A   Electrolysis

   B   Phytoextraction

   C   Reduction with carbon

   [1]

4. Atoms have no overall charge because...

   A   ...they contain neutrons.

   B   ...they have an even number of protons.

   C   ...they contain equal numbers of protons. and electrons.

   [1]

5. What happens during the sedimentation step of water purification?

   A   Chemicals are added to the water that cause particles to clump together and sink to the bottom.

   B   The water is passed through a wire mesh.

   C   The water is treated to kill harmful bacteria and other microbes.

   [1]

6. Brass is an alloy of zinc and copper. Why is brass stronger than pure copper?

   A   Zinc has a lower density than copper.

   B   Zinc is more reactive than copper.

   C   Zinc atoms are a different size to copper atoms, so it is harder for the layers of atoms to slide over each other.

   [1]

7. True or False? "A solution with a pH of 1 is very acidic."

   A   True

   B   False

   [1]

8. True or False? "When forming an ionic bond, metal atoms generally lose electrons to form positive ions."

   A   True

   B   False

   [1]

Mixed Tests for Paper 1

9. Copper has two stable isotopes, copper-63 and copper-65.
   Copper-63 has an abundance of 69.2%.
   Copper-65 has an abundance of 30.8%.

   Calculate the relative atomic mass of copper.
   Give your answer to three significant figures.

   ....

   ....

   ....

   Relative atomic mass = ...
   [2]

10. Explain why metals that are lower in the reactivity series are cheaper to extract than those that are higher up in the reactivity series.

    ....

    ....

    ....

    ....
    [3]

11. The theoretical yield of product X from a reaction is 81 g. The actual yield is 59 g.
    Calculate the percentage yield of product X.

    ....

    ....

    Percentage yield = ... %
    [2]

Test 16: Paper 1 Mixed Topics

There are **12 questions** in this test. Give yourself **10 minutes** to answer them all.

1. Which is the correct, balanced ionic equation for the displacement of calcium ions by sodium?

   A $Na_{(s)} + Ca^{2+}_{(aq)} \rightarrow Na^+_{(aq)} + Ca_{(s)}$

   B $Na_{(s)} + Ca^{2+}_{(aq)} \rightarrow Na^{2+}_{(aq)} + Ca_{(s)}$

   C $2Na_{(s)} + Ca^{2+}_{(aq)} \rightarrow 2Na^+_{(aq)} + Ca_{(s)}$

   [1]

2. True or False? "Potable water is any water that is safe enough to drink."

   A   True

   B   False

   [1]

3. Which process can be used to find the amount of acid required to neutralise a given quantity of alkali?

   A   Titration

   B   Distillation

   C   Electrolysis

   [1]

4. What is the formula of a nitrate ion?

   A   NO

   B NO_3^-

   C N^{3-}

   [1]

5. What is the chemical test for hydrogen?

   A   It burns with a green flame.

   B   It turns damp litmus paper white.

   C   It burns with a squeaky pop.

   [1]

6. Which of these best describes a metallic structure?

   A   A giant structure of metal atoms held together by ionic bonds.

   B   A giant structure of metal atoms arranged in an irregular pattern.

   C   A giant structure of metal ions arranged in a regular pattern.

   [1]

7. Which of the following statements about solids is false?

   A   The particles have high energies.

   B   There are strong forces of attraction between the particles.

   C   They keep a definite volume.

   [1]

8. True or False? "Simple distillation can be used to separate mixtures of liquids with similar boiling points."

   A   True

   B   False

   [1]

9. What is electrolysis?

   ....

   ....
   [1]

10. Reversible reactions can reach 'dynamic equilibrium'. What is meant by this?

    ....

    ....
    [1]

11. An element has the electronic configuration 2. 8. 4.

    Which group of the periodic table must it be in? Explain your answer.

    ....

    ....
    [2]

12. The Haber process uses an exothermic reaction to produce ammonia.
    Explain why the reaction is carried out at a moderately high temperature (450 °C).

    ....

    ....

    ....

    ....
    [3]

Test 17: Groups in the Periodic Table

There are **12 questions** in this test. Give yourself **10 minutes** to answer them all.

1. True or False? "The further down Group 7 you go, the more reactive the elements get."
   - A True
   - B False

   [1]

2. What is the name for the elements in Group 0 of the periodic table?
   - A Alkali metals
   - B Halogens
   - C Noble gases

   [1]

3. When lithium reacts with water, the resulting solution is...
   - A ...acidic.
   - B ...alkaline.
   - C ...neutral.

   [1]

4. At room temperature, chlorine (Cl_2) is a...
   - A ...yellow liquid.
   - B ...orange gas.
   - C ...green gas.

   [1]

5. True or False? "Alkali metals are soft."
   - A True
   - B False

   [1]

6. Halogen displacement reactions are examples of...
   - A ...neutralisation reactions.
   - B ...combustion reactions.
   - C ...redox reactions.

   [1]

7. How do the melting points of the alkali metals compare with those of other metals?
   - A They are higher than other metals.
   - B They are lower than other metals.
   - C They are the same as other metals.

   [1]

8. Which Group 7 element is a dark grey crystalline solid at room temperature?
   - A Fluorine
   - B Bromine
   - C Iodine

   [1]

Topics for Paper 2: Groups in the Periodic Table

9. Explain, in terms of reactivity, why a displacement reaction can occur when a halogen is added to a halide salt.

....

....
[1]

10. Why do Group 1 elements become more reactive as you go down the group?

....

....

....
[2]

11. Explain, in terms of electronic configuration, why the noble gases are inert.

....

....

....
[2]

12. Write a balanced symbol equation for the reaction between chlorine and sodium metal. Include state symbols.

....
[2]

15

Topics for Paper 2: Groups in the Periodic Table

Test 18: Groups in the Periodic Table

There are **11 questions** in this test. Give yourself **10 minutes** to answer them all.

1. The first three elements of Group 7 are fluorine, chlorine and bromine. Which is the most reactive?

   A Bromine
   B Chlorine
   C Fluorine
   [1]

2. What happens to the boiling points of the elements as you go down Group 0?

   A They decrease
   B They increase
   C They remain constant
   [1]

3. Which of these is a chemical test for chlorine?

   A It burns with a squeaky pop.
   B It turns damp blue litmus paper white.
   C It turns bromine water colourless.
   [1]

4. In which group of the periodic table would you find the alkali metals?

   A Group 0
   B Group 1
   C Group 2
   [1]

5. Which of the following halogens has the lowest melting point?

   A Bromine
   B Chlorine
   C Iodine
   [1]

6. Hydrogen halides dissolve in water to form...

   A ...neutral solutions.
   B ...basic solutions.
   C ...acidic solutions.
   [1]

7. Which of the following statements about noble gases is false?

   A They are all yellow gases.
   B They are all inert.
   C They are all monatomic.
   [1]

8. Which of the following reacts the most vigorously with water?

   A Lithium
   B Potassium
   C Sodium
   [1]

Topics for Paper 2: Groups in the Periodic Table

9. Give **one** property of helium that makes it a suitable gas for use in a balloon.
   Explain your answer.

   ....

   ....

   ....
   [2]

10. When chlorine is added to potassium bromide, the following reaction occurs:

    $$Cl_2 + 2KBr \rightarrow Br_2 + 2KCl$$

    Identify the substance that is reduced and the substance that is oxidised in this reaction.

    Reduced: ....

    Oxidised: ....
    [2]

11. Describe and explain the trend in the reactivity of the halogens down the group.

    ....

    ....

    ....

    ....

    ....
    [3]

15

Test 19: Rates of Reaction and Energy Changes

There are **11 questions** in this test. Give yourself **10 minutes** to answer them all.

1. To break a chemical bond...

   A ...energy must be supplied.

   B ...energy must be released.
   [1]

2. How does a catalyst increase a reaction's rate?

   A It shifts the position of equilibrium.

   B It increases the energy of the reactants.

   C It decreases the activation energy needed.
   [1]

3. True or False? "The rate of reaction can be found by measuring the amount of reactant used over a period of time."

   A True

   B False
   [1]

4. True or False? "In a reaction between gases, increasing the pressure of the reaction mixture will increase the reaction rate."

   A True

   B False
   [1]

5. The rate of a reaction doesn't depend on the...

   A ...frequency of collisions.

   B ...volume of solution.

   C ...temperature of the reactants.
   [1]

6. Which of the following can be used to measure the energy change when a chemical reaction takes place?

   A Change in colour

   B Change in mass

   C Change in temperature
   [1]

7. Which of the following affects the proportion of collisions that have enough energy for particles to react?

   A Gas pressure

   B Temperature

   C Concentration
   [1]

8. What is the activation energy of a reaction?

   A The total energy of the reactants.

   B The minimum amount of energy needed by the particles to react.

   C The maximum amount of energy needed by the particles to react.
   [1]

Topics for Paper 2: Rates of Reaction and Energy Changes

9. The diagram shows the results of the same reaction carried out in two different experiments.

Suggest **one** way in which the conditions in experiment 2 could have been different to those in experiment 1. Explain your answer.

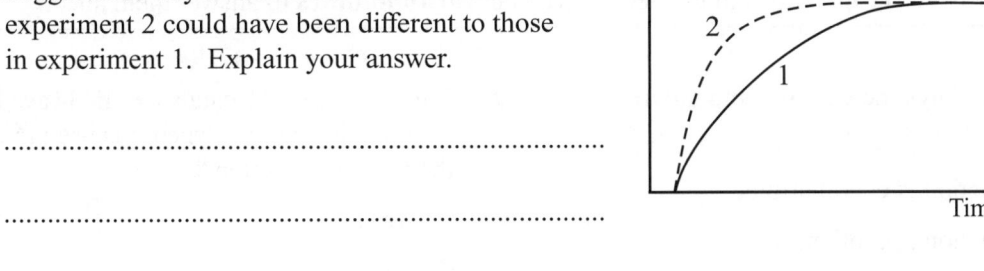

....

....

....
[2]

10. Marble chips react with hydrochloric acid to form calcium chloride, water and carbon dioxide. Describe how you could determine the average rate of this reaction.

....

....

....

....
[3]

11. Does the reaction profile on the right show an exothermic or an endothermic reaction? Explain your answer.

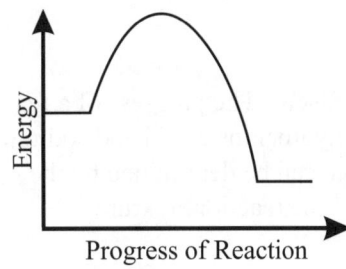

....

....
[2]

Test 20: Rates of Reaction and Energy Changes

There are **11 questions** in this test. Give yourself **10 minutes** to answer them all.

1. If the surroundings increase in temperature during a reaction...

   A ...the reaction is endothermic.

   B ...the reaction is exothermic.

   C ...no new chemical bonds have formed.
   [1]

2. True or False? "A catalyst will always be chemically changed when it is used to increase the rate of a reaction."

   A True

   B False
   [1]

3. In a reaction between marble and hydrochloric acid, using small marble chips instead of a large piece of marble will produce...

   A ...no difference in the rate of reaction.

   B ...a faster rate of reaction.

   C ...a slower rate of reaction.
   [1]

4. In an endothermic reaction, the products are at...

   A ...a lower energy than the reactants.

   B ...a higher energy than the reactants.
   [1]

5. In an endothermic reaction, the energy released when bonds are formed is...

   A ...less than the energy used in breaking old bonds.

   B ...greater than the energy used in breaking old bonds.
   [1]

6. On a graph showing the quantity of product formed against time, a tangent to the curve can be used to find the...

   A ...concentration of the product.

   B ...mean rate of reaction.

   C ...rate of reaction at a specific time.
   [1]

7. True or False? "The progress of a reaction between hydrochloric acid and sodium thiosulfate can be determined by the colour change of the reaction mixture."

   A True

   B False
   [1]

8. Which of the following is a reason why increasing the temperature increases the rate of a reaction?

   A The higher temperature reduces the activation energy.

   B The reactant particles move faster so they collide more frequently.

   C The reactant particles expand so they collide more frequently.
   [1]

Topics for Paper 2: Rates of Reaction and Energy Changes

9. Explain, in terms of particle collisions, why increasing the concentration of reacting solutions increases the rate of a reaction.

....

....

....
[2]

10. The equation below shows the combustion of methane.

$$CH_4 + 2O_2 \rightarrow CO_2 + 2H_2O$$

The structures of methane, oxygen, carbon dioxide and water are shown below.

Using the bond energies below, work out the overall energy change for the combustion of methane.

C–H: 413 kJ mol^{-1}, O=O: 496 kJ mol^{-1}, C=O: 803 kJ mol^{-1}, O–H: 464 kJ mol^{-1}

....

....

....

....

.... kJ mol^{-1}
[4]

11. State the function of yeast in the fermentation process used to produce alcoholic drinks.

....

....
[1]

Test 21: Fuels and Earth Science

There are **11 questions** in this test. Give yourself **10 minutes** to answer them all.

1. Crude oil is...

   A ...a renewable resource.

   B ...a finite resource.

   C ...an infinite resource.
   [1]

2. Why might sulfur impurities be removed from a fuel before it is burnt?

   A So the fuel produces less soot when it burns.

   B To reduce the cost of the fuel.

   C To reduce emissions which cause acid rain.
   [1]

3. Which of these gases is **not** a greenhouse gas?

   A Water vapour

   B Methane

   C Nitrogen
   [1]

4. Carbon monoxide is...

   A ...a toxic gas.

   B ...a hydrocarbon.

   C ...a fuel.
   [1]

5. Which technique is used to separate the components of crude oil?

   A Cracking

   B Filtration

   C Fractional distillation
   [1]

6. Which of the following is **not** a use of the fuel oil fraction of crude oil?

   A Fuel for some power stations

   B Fuel for aircraft

   C Fuel for large ships
   [1]

7. The Earth's oceans were formed by...

   A ...melting of prehistoric ice caps.

   B ...earthquakes releasing liquid water trapped beneath the Earth's surface.

   C ...condensation of water vapour that was present in the early atmosphere.
   [1]

8. True or False? "Short-chain hydrocarbons are generally more useful than long-chain hydrocarbons."

   A True

   B False
   [1]

Topics for Paper 2: Fuels and Earth Science

9. Which gas is thought to have made up most of the Earth's early atmosphere?

   ....

   Name **one** other gas present in the Earth's early atmosphere.

   ....

   Where are these gases thought to have come from?

   ....
   [3]

10. Decane and icosane are two alkanes.
    Decane has the molecular formula $C_{10}H_{22}$. Icosane has the molecular formula $C_{20}H_{42}$.
    Predict which of these two alkanes has the lower viscosity. Explain your answer.

    ....

    ....

    ....
    [2]

11. Give **one** human activity that increases the amount of carbon dioxide in the atmosphere.
    Explain why it causes an increase.

    ....

    ....

    ....
    [2]

Topics for Paper 2: Fuels and Earth Science

Test 22: Fuels and Earth Science

There are **11 questions** in this test. Give yourself **10 minutes** to answer them all.

1. True or False? "Cracking is used to turn long-chain hydrocarbons into short-chain hydrocarbons."

   A True
   B False
   [1]

2. True or False? "All hydrocarbons contain carbon and hydrogen, but some hydrocarbons also contain oxygen."

   A True
   B False
   [1]

3. Which of these is thought to be increasing the average global temperature?

   A An increasing amount of greenhouse gases in the atmosphere.
   B A decreased amount of water vapour in the atmosphere.
   C Large amounts of sulfur dioxide gas being released from burning fuels.
   [1]

4. When the oceans formed, the amount of CO_2 in the atmosphere...

   A ...increased.
   B ...stayed the same.
   C ...decreased.
   [1]

5. True or False? "Nitrogen oxides can be formed by the chemical reactions in car engines."

   A True
   B False
   [1]

6. Which of the following does **not** vary for different members of the same homologous series of compounds?

   A Boiling point
   B General formula
   C Length of molecule
   [1]

7. Which of the following is a crude oil fraction that is used to surface roads?

   A Bitumen
   B Diesel oil
   C Kerosene
   [1]

8. Which of these is **not** produced when a fuel undergoes complete combustion?

   A Carbon monoxide
   B Carbon dioxide
   C Water
   [1]

Topics for Paper 2: Fuels and Earth Science

9. Vaporised crude oil is piped into the bottom of a fractionating column. Explain how it is then separated into different fractions.

   ....

   ....

   ....

   ....

   .... *[3]*

10. Hydrogen gas can be used as a fuel to power vehicles. Give **one** advantage and **one** disadvantage of using hydrogen instead of petrol as a fuel for cars.

    Advantage: ....

    ....

    Disadvantage: ....

    .... *[2]*

11. Describe how the evolution of green plants affected the composition of Earth's atmosphere. Name the process which caused this change.

    ....

    ....

    .... *[2]*

Test 23: Separate Chemistry 2

There are **12 questions** in this test. Give yourself **10 minutes** to answer them all.

1. True or False? "Nanoparticles have a very low surface area to volume ratio."

   A True
   B False
   [1]

2. What is the formula of ethane?

   A C_2H_4
   B C_2H_6
   C C_3H_6
   [1]

3. What solutions are normally used to test for sulfate ions?

   A Dilute hydrochloric acid and barium chloride solution.
   B Dilute nitric acid and barium chloride solution.
   [1]

4. What happens to bromine water when an alkene is added to it?

   A It turns cloudy.
   B It turns from colourless to orange.
   C It turns from orange to colourless.
   [1]

5. What colour is the flame produced when a calcium compound is burnt in a flame test?

   A Green
   B Orange-red
   C Yellow
   [1]

6. Which of these is not an alcohol?

   A Methanol
   B Butane
   C Propanol
   [1]

7. What happens to the carbon and hydrogen in a hydrocarbon when it's burned?

   A They are oxidised.
   B They evaporate.
   C They react to form CH_4.
   [1]

8. What gas will be released when dilute hydrochloric acid is added to a solution of sodium carbonate?

   A Hydrogen
   B Carbon dioxide
   C Methane
   [1]

Topics for Paper 2: Separate Chemistry 2

9. Give **two** advantages of using instrumental analysis, such as flame photometry, instead of chemical tests to identify unknown substances.

   1. ....

   2. ....
   [2]

10. A student carried out a series of tests on an unknown compound.

    Here are the results of the tests:

    Adding sodium hydroxide to a solution of the compound produced a green precipitate.

    Adding dilute nitric acid and then silver nitrate to a solution of the compound produced a cream precipitate.

    Identify:

    the metal ion present in the compound ....

    the non-metal ion present in the compound ....
    [2]

11. Why are alkenes described as unsaturated?

    ....

    ....
    [1]

12. Give **one** use of nanoparticles.
    Explain what property of nanoparticles makes them suitable for that use.

    ....

    ....
    [2]

15

Test 24: Separate Chemistry 2

There are **11 questions** in this test. Give yourself **10 minutes** to answer them all.

1. Which of these metal ions forms a blue precipitate in a reaction with sodium hydroxide solution?

   A   Iron(III) ions

   B   Copper(II) ions

   C   Iron(II) ions

   [1]

2. When ethanol is oxidised, it produces...

   A   ...an ester.

   B   ...ethanoic acid.

   C   ...sodium polymer.

   [1]

3. True or False? "Condensation polymerisation involves monomers with a single functional group."

   A   True

   B   False

   [1]

4. What is DNA?

   A   A molecule with an amino group and a carboxyl group.

   B   A polymer made up of amino acids.

   C   A polymer made up of monomers called nucleotides.

   [1]

5. Which of the following statements about using a flame photometer is true?

   A   It cannot be used to identify the concentration of ions in solution.

   B   It can identify several metal ions in a substance.

   C   It can only be used to identify non-metal ions.

   [1]

6. What is produced when an aqueous solution of carbohydrates is fermented using yeast?

   A   Aqueous ethene and carbon dioxide

   B   Nitrogen and aqueous ethanol

   C   Carbon dioxide and aqueous ethanol

   [1]

7. Which statement about nanoparticles is true?

   A   Nanoparticles are smaller than atoms.

   B   Nanoparticles are larger than simple molecules.

   C   Nanoparticles are larger than atoms, but smaller than simple molecules.

   [1]

8. What is the functional group of an alcohol?

   A   –OH

   B   –C=O

   C   –COOH

   [1]

Topics for Paper 2: Separate Chemistry 2

9. How could you use sodium hydroxide to distinguish between solutions of aluminium chloride and calcium chloride?

....

....

....
[2]

10. PVDF is an addition polymer which is used to insulate electrical wires. The formula of PVDF is shown on the right.

    Draw the displayed formula of the monomer used to make PVDF.

    $$\left(\begin{array}{c} H \\ | \\ -C- \\ | \\ H \end{array} \begin{array}{c} F \\ | \\ C- \\ | \\ F \end{array}\right)_n$$

[1]

11. A local council is trying to reduce the amount of polymer waste it sends to landfill. The councillors are evaluating two alternative options to dispose of polymers. The two options are recycling and disposal by combustion.
    Suggest **one** advantage and **one** disadvantage for each option.

....

....

....

....

....

....

....
[4]

15

Test 25: Separate Chemistry 2

There are **11 questions** in this test. Give yourself **10 minutes** to answer them all.

1. What colour is silver iodide?

   A Cream
   B White
   C Yellow
   [1]

2. When a polyester forms...

   A ...double bonds in the monomers open up.
   B ...carbon dioxide is given off.
   C ...water molecules are also formed.
   [1]

3. Which of the following sets of properties would describe the most suitable polymer for a lemonade bottle?

   A strong, mouldable, high density
   B low density, brittle, electrical insulator
   C mouldable, flexible, unreactive
   [1]

4. In a flame test, which metal compounds burn to give a yellow flame?

   A Calcium
   B Potassium
   C Sodium
   [1]

5. How many C–C single bonds are there in one molecule of propene?

   A 0
   B 1
   C 2
   [1]

6. True or False? "Nanoparticles have different properties compared with bulk amounts of the same material."

   A True
   B False
   [1]

7. What are the monomers that make up proteins?

   A Amino acids
   B Nucleotides
   C Sugars
   [1]

8. When testing a gas with litmus paper, what would you expect to observe if ammonia is present?

   A Damp litmus paper turns white.
   B Damp red litmus paper turns blue.
   C Damp blue litmus paper turns red.
   [1]

Topics for Paper 2: Separate Chemistry 2

9. Name the type of reaction shown on the right and explain why ethene can undergo this reaction.

$$n \begin{pmatrix} H & H \\ | & | \\ C = C \\ | & | \\ H & H \end{pmatrix} \longrightarrow \begin{pmatrix} H & H \\ | & | \\ -C - C- \\ | & | \\ H & H \end{pmatrix}_n$$

ethene $\longrightarrow$ poly(ethene)

....

....

[2]

10. Some properties of three materials are summarised in the table.

Material	Strength	Corrosion resistance	Cost
A	Medium	High	High
B	High	Low	Low
C	Low	Medium	Medium

Using the information in the table, explain why material A is used to make medical instruments while materials B and C are not used for this purpose. Discuss strength, corrosion resistance and cost in your answer.

....

....

....

....

[3]

11. A molecule of an organic compound is shown on the right.

$$\begin{matrix} & H & H & H & H & H & H & H \\ & | & | & | & | & | & | & | \\ H- & C - C - C - C - C - C - C - O - H \\ & | & | & | & | & | & | & | \\ & H & H & H & H & H & H & H \end{matrix}$$

Predict the type of compound formed when this molecule is oxidised. Explain your answer.

....

....

[2]

Mixed Tests for Paper 2

Test 26: Paper 2 Mixed Topics

There are **11 questions** in this test. Give yourself **10 minutes** to answer them all.

1. In which group of the periodic table would you find the halogens?

   A Group 1

   B Group 6

   C Group 7

   [1]

2. True or False? "Chemical reactions all happen at the same speed."

   A True

   B False

   [1]

3. Which of the following is **not** a reason that carbon dioxide levels decreased in the Earth's early atmosphere?

   A Lots of carbon dioxide dissolved into the oceans.

   B The carbon dioxide reacted with oxygen in the atmosphere.

   C Green plants began to photosynthesise.

   [1]

4. Which of the following statements about polymers is false?

   A They always contain carbon-carbon double bonds.

   B They have a high average relative molecular mass.

   C They're made up of lots of small repeating units.

   [1]

5. True or False? "Oxygen will relight a glowing splint."

   A True

   B False

   [1]

6. An element has a mass number of 23 and an atomic number of 11. How many neutrons are there in an atom of this element?

   A 11

   B 12

   C 23

   [1]

7. You can test for halide ions by adding dilute nitric acid to a solution followed by...

   A ...limewater.

   B ...silver nitrate solution.

   C ...sodium hydroxide solution.

   [1]

8. When a pair of electrons is shared between two atoms...

   A ...an ionic bond is formed.

   B ...the atoms become charged.

   C ...a covalent bond is formed.

   [1]

9. Give **one** possible human health risk associated with the use of nanoparticles.

   ....

   ....
   [1]

10. The formulas of two alkanes, decane and pentane, are shown below:

    Decane: $C_{10}H_{22}$

    Pentane: C_5H_{12}

    Which of these alkanes will have the higher boiling point?
    Explain your answer.

    ....

    ....

    ....

    ....
    [2]

11. 200 g of calcium reacts with exactly 80 g of oxygen gas (O_2) to give calcium oxide. Calcium oxide is an ionic compound and the only product formed in this reaction. Use the masses and relative atomic masses provided to write a balanced symbol equation for this reaction.

    Relative atomic masses (A_r): O = 16, Ca = 40

    ....

    ....

    ....

    ....

    Symbol equation: ....
    [4]

Test 27: Paper 2 Mixed Topics

There are **11 questions** in this test. Give yourself **10 minutes** to answer them all.

1. Why is cracking of hydrocarbons carried out?
   - A To purify the fractions of crude oil.
   - B To generate electricity.
   - C To convert long alkane molecules into smaller, more useful molecules.

   [1]

2. Propene can combine with other propene molecules to form poly(propene). What sort of reaction is this?
   - A Condensation polymerisation
   - B Addition polymerisation
   - C Combustion

   [1]

3. Which of the following statements about catalysts is true?
   - A They don't alter the products of a reaction.
   - B They increase the yield of a reaction.
   - C They are used up in a reaction.

   [1]

4. True or False? "The more solute there is in a given volume the less concentrated the solution is."
   - A True
   - B False

   [1]

5. When chlorine displaces iodine from a solution of potassium iodide, chlorine...
   - A ...gains electrons.
   - B ...loses electrons.
   - C ...gains oxygen.

   [1]

6. Which of the following is used to test for the presence of an alkene?
   - A Limewater
   - B Bromine water
   - C Sodium hydroxide solution

   [1]

7. If a reaction takes in heat energy from the surroundings, the products of the reaction have...
   - A ...more energy than the reactants.
   - B ...less energy than the reactants.
   - C ...equal energy to the reactants.

   [1]

8. Why is carbon monoxide a dangerous pollutant?
   - A It stops the blood carrying oxygen around the body.
   - B It causes acid rain.
   - C It builds up in the lungs and blocks the airways.

   [1]

9. 1.84 g of ethanol (C₂H₅OH) is burnt completely in oxygen.
Calculate the number of moles of carbon dioxide gas produced.

$$C_2H_5OH + 3O_2 \rightarrow 2CO_2 + 3H_2O$$

Relative formula mass (M_r) of C_2H_5OH = 46.

....

....

.... mol
[2]

10. Explain how the bonding in graphite makes it a suitable material for electrodes.

....

....

....

....
[3]

11. A student stands a flask containing hydrochloric acid over a black cross. She adds some sodium thiosulfate solution and measures the time taken for the solution to turn cloudy enough for the black cross to disappear.

She repeats the experiment at a higher temperature.
Predict the effect that increased temperature will have on the amount of time taken for the black cross to disappear. Explain your answer.

....

....

....
[2]

15

Test 28: Paper 2 Mixed Topics

There are **11 questions** in this test. Give yourself **10 minutes** to answer them all.

1. True or False? "Oxides of nitrogen are harmful pollutants."

    A   True

    B   False

    [1]

2. A white precipitate is formed when dilute nitric acid and then silver nitrate solution are added to a solution. What does this show?

    A   The solution contains chloride ions.

    B   The solution contains iodide ions.

    C   The solution contains bromide ions.

    [1]

3. Why can the relative reactivity of lithium, sodium and potassium be used to predict the relative reactivity of rubidium?

    A   Because they are in the same group of the periodic table.

    B   Because they have similar atomic radii.

    C   Because all metals react in the same way.

    [1]

4. Carbon and carbon monoxide can be produced in combustion reactions where...

    A   ...there is not enough nitrogen.

    B   ...there is not enough fuel.

    C   ...there is not enough oxygen.

    [1]

5. Why can the hydrocarbons in crude oil be separated by fractional distillation?

    A   They have different boiling points.

    B   They have different melting points.

    C   They have different viscosities.

    [1]

6. In an exothermic reaction the energy required to break bonds is...

    A   ...less than the energy released when new bonds form.

    B   ...greater than the energy released when new bonds form.

    [1]

7. In a flame test, a blue-green flame would show that the compound contained...

    A   ...copper ions.

    B   ...calcium ions.

    C   ...potassium ions.

    [1]

8. True or False? "Atoms of the same element always have the same number of neutrons."

    A   True

    B   False

    [1]

9. Using collision theory, explain how breaking a solid reactant up into smaller pieces will affect the rate of a reaction.

   ....
   ....
   ....
   ....
   ....
   [3]

10. A student is carrying out an experiment to determine which alcohol (ethanol, propanol, butanol or pentanol) is the most efficient fuel.
    He burns a sample of each alcohol in a spirit burner and measures the mass of each alcohol required to raise the temperature of a sample of water by 20 °C. The table shows his results.

Fuel	Ethanol	Propanol	Butanol	Pentanol
Mass of fuel used (g)	0.51	0.42	0.33	0.27

    Which alcohol is the most efficient fuel?

    ....
    [1]

11. A 53.8 g sample of copper chloride contains 25.4 g of copper and 28.4 g of chlorine. Calculate the empirical formula of copper chloride.

    Relative atomic masses (A_r): Cl = 35.5, Cu = 63.5

    ....
    ....
    ....
    ....
    ....
    [3]

Test 29: Paper 2 Mixed Topics

There are **12 questions** in this test. Give yourself **10 minutes** to answer them all.

1. Which of the following statements about crude oil is false?

   A   It is a finite resource.

   B   It is a mixture of ionic compounds.

   C   It can be separated by fractional distillation.

   [1]

2. CH_4 and Cl_2 are...

   A   ...simple molecules.

   B   ...polymers.

   C   ...giant covalent structures.

   [1]

3. How are polyesters formed?

   A   Addition polymerisation

   B   Condensation polymerisation

   C   Cracking

   [1]

4. Halogen X will displace halogen Y from an aqueous solution of its salt if halogen X is...

   A   ...more reactive than halogen Y.

   B   ...less reactive than halogen Y.

   [1]

5. An alkali metal, M, is added to some water. M fizzes, melts and produces a flame. Which of the following metals is M most likely to be?

   A   Lithium

   B   Sodium

   C   Potassium

   [1]

6. Displacement reactions between a metal and a metal compound...

   A   ...are exothermic.

   B   ...are endothermic.

   C   ...do not involve a change in heat energy.

   [1]

7. Which of the following would you need to calculate the energy change of a reaction?

   A   The energies of the reactant bonds only.

   B   The energies of the product bonds only.

   C   The energies of both the reactant and the product bonds.

   [1]

8. True or False? "Carbon dioxide is the most abundant gas in the atmosphere today."

   A   True

   B   False

   [1]

Mixed Tests for Paper 2

9. The relative atomic mass of chlorine is 35.5.
   Explain why the relative atomic mass of chlorine is not a whole number.

   ....

   ....

   ....
   [2]

10. Explain why the chemical test for any ion must be unique.

    ....

    ....
    [1]

11. Give **one** reason why ceramics make good building materials.

    ....

    ....
    [1]

12. The equation for the formation of ammonia is: $N_2 + 3H_2 \rightarrow 2NH_3$
    The overall energy change of this reaction is -97 kJ mol^{-1}.
    Draw and label a reaction profile for this reaction on the axes below.
    Label the overall energy change.

    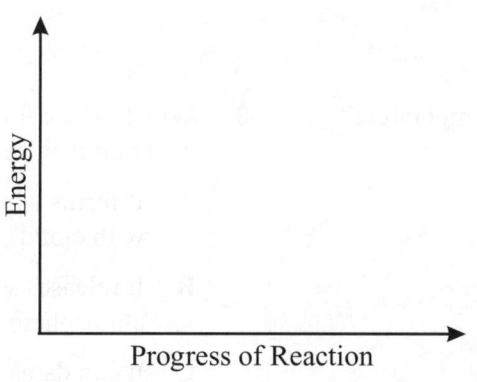

    [3]

Test 30: Paper 2 Mixed Topics

There are **11 questions** in this test. Give yourself **10 minutes** to answer them all.

1. True or False? "Catalysts are used up during a reaction."

   A True

   B False

   [1]

2. Which of the following are produced by cracking?

   A Alkanes and water vapour

   B Alkanes and alkenes

   C Only alkenes

   [1]

3. How many molecules of CO_2 are in one mole?

   A 44

   B 1

   C 6.02×10^{23}

   [1]

4. Which of the following will increase the rate of reaction between two aqueous solutions?

   A Diluting the solutions.

   B Using a bigger reaction vessel.

   C Increasing the average energy of the collisions.

   [1]

5. When a chemical bond forms...

   A ...energy must be supplied.

   B ...energy is released.

   [1]

6. The discovery of the electron led to the...

   A ...plum pudding atomic model.

   B ...Bohr atomic model.

   C ...currently accepted version of the atom.

   [1]

7. What colour is bromine at room temperature?

   A Red-brown

   B Purple

   C Cream

   [1]

8. Which of the following statements about acid rain is false?

   A It forms when sulfur dioxide mixes with clouds.

   B It releases soot into the atmosphere.

   C It can damage stone statues.

   [1]

Mixed Tests for Paper 2

9. Describe how greenhouse gases cause the warming of the surface of the Earth.

....

....

....

....

....
[4]

10. Give the name of the compound shown below.

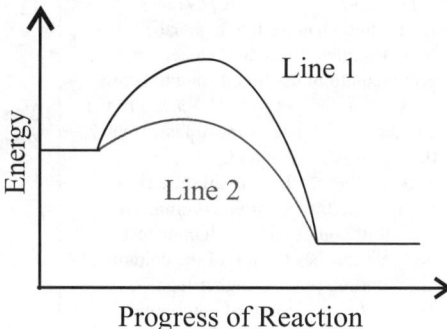

....
[1]

11. A certain reaction is carried out with and without a catalyst.
Which line on the graph shows the reaction with a catalyst? Explain your answer.

....

....

....
[2]

Answers

Key Concepts in Chemistry

Test 1: Key Concepts in Chemistry
Pages 2–3
1. C *[1 mark]*
2. A *[1 mark]*
3. C *[1 mark]*
4. C *[1 mark]*
5. C *[1 mark]*
6. B *[1 mark]*
7. C *[1 mark]*
8. B *[1 mark]*
9. They have the same number of outer electrons/electrons in their outer shell *[1 mark]*
10. $2Li + 2H_2O \rightarrow 2LiOH + H_2$ *[1 mark]*
11. Number of moles of C = 66 g ÷ 12 = 5.5
    From balanced equation, 5.5 moles of CO_2 are produced *[1 mark]*.
    Relative formula mass (M_r) of CO_2
    = 12 + (2 × 16) = 44 *[1 mark]*.
    Mass of CO_2 = moles × M_r
    = 5.5 × 44 = 242 g *[1 mark]*
    [Or 3 marks for the correct answer via any other method.]
12. The two oxygen atoms share two pairs of electrons *[1 mark]*.
    This forms a double covalent bond *[1 mark]*.

Test 2: Key Concepts in Chemistry
Pages 4–5
1. A *[1 mark]*
2. B *[1 mark]*
3. A *[1 mark]*
4. B *[1 mark]*
5. A *[1 mark]*
6. A *[1 mark]*
7. B *[1 mark]*
8. B *[1 mark]*
9. Isotopes are atoms of the same element, which have the same number of protons but a different number of neutrons *[1 mark]*
10. 0.00025 kg × 1000 = 0.25 g
    Concentration = mass ÷ volume
    = 0.25 ÷ 0.5 *[1 mark]*
    = 0.5 g dm^{-3} *[1 mark]*
    [Or 2 marks for the correct answer via any other method.]
11. The structure is made up of positive (sodium) ions and negative (chloride) ions in a regular arrangement *[1 mark]*.
    The structure is held together by ionic bonds/electrostatic forces between the oppositely charged ions *[1 mark]*.
12. Graphite has free/delocalised electrons *[1 mark]* that can move *[1 mark]*.

Test 3: Key Concepts in Chemistry
Pages 6–7
1. A *[1 mark]*
2. B *[1 mark]*
3. B *[1 mark]*
4. A *[1 mark]*
5. C *[1 mark]*
6. C *[1 mark]*
7. A *[1 mark]*
8. C *[1 mark]*
9. Each Group 1 atom loses an electron to form a positively-charged ion and each Group 7 atom gains one electron to form a negatively-charged ion *[1 mark]*.
10. Carbon nanotubes are tiny cylinders made from a single layer of carbon atoms / graphene *[1 mark]*. The carbon atoms are joined together in hexagons *[1 mark]*. They can conduct electricity because they contain delocalised electrons *[1 mark]*.
11. Relative formula mass (M_r)
    = 32 + (2 × 16) = 64 *[1 mark]*
    number of moles = mass ÷ M_r
    = 160 ÷ 64 = 2.5 moles *[1 mark]*
    Number of molecules
    = 2.5 × 6.02 × 10^{23}
    = 1.505 × 10^{24} *[1 mark]*
    [Or 3 marks for the correct answer via any other method.]

Topics for Paper 1

Test 4: States of Matter and Mixtures
Pages 8–9
1. B *[1 mark]*
2. C *[1 mark]*
3. B *[1 mark]*
4. B *[1 mark]*
5. A *[1 mark]*
6. B *[1 mark]*
7. C *[1 mark]*
8. A *[1 mark]*
9. As a liquid changes into a gas, the particles move from their close, irregular arrangement in the liquid state to being far apart in the gas state *[1 mark]*. In the gas state, the particles move faster than in the liquid state *[1 mark]*.
10. Vapour from the boiling mixture rises through the fractionating column. Any vapour of compound 1 will condense before it reaches the top of the column as its boiling point is higher than 70 °C *[1 mark]*. The vapour of compound 2 will not condense in the column, as its boiling point is lower than 70 °C *[1 mark]*. This means only the vapour of compound 2 will reach the condenser and be collected, separating compound 2 from compound 1 in the flask *[1 mark]*.
11. A pure substance will always leave a single spot on the chromatography paper *[1 mark]*. An impure substance will usually leave multiple spots *[1 mark]*.

Test 5: States of Matter and Mixtures
Pages 10–11
1. B *[1 mark]*
2. C *[1 mark]*
3. A *[1 mark]*
4. B *[1 mark]*
5. A *[1 mark]*
6. A *[1 mark]*
7. C *[1 mark]*
8. B *[1 mark]*
9. R_f = 3.2 ÷ 4.9
    = 0.6530... *[1 mark]*
    = 0.65 (to 2 s.f.) *[1 mark]*
10. Ethanol (it boils at 78°C) *[1 mark]*
11. Place a spot of the ink on a starting line, marked in pencil, near the bottom of a strip of filter paper *[1 mark]*. Place the bottom of the filter paper in a beaker containing a small amount of solvent *[1 mark]* so the ink is above the solvent level *[1 mark]*.
12. E.g. the ice/water is impure *[1 mark]*.

Test 6: Chemical Changes
Pages 12–13
1. C *[1 mark]*
2. A *[1 mark]*
3. A *[1 mark]*
4. B *[1 mark]*
5. B *[1 mark]*
6. C *[1 mark]*
7. C *[1 mark]*
8. B *[1 mark]*
9. Hydrogen gas *[1 mark]*, because e.g. sodium is more reactive than hydrogen *[1 mark]*. Chlorine gas *[1 mark]*, because e.g. chloride ions are present in the solution *[1 mark]*.
10. $H^+_{(aq)} + OH^-_{(aq)} \rightarrow H_2O_{(l)}$ *[1 mark]*
11. E.g. to make sure all the acid has reacted. / To make sure there is no leftover acid in the product *[1 mark]*.
12. Bubble the gas through the limewater. If the gas is carbon dioxide, the limewater will turn cloudy white/milky *[1 mark]*.

Test 7: Chemical Changes
Pages 14–15
1. A *[1 mark]*
2. C *[1 mark]*
3. A *[1 mark]*
4. A *[1 mark]*
5. B *[1 mark]*
6. C *[1 mark]*
7. A *[1 mark]*
8. C *[1 mark]*
9. zinc sulfate *[1 mark]*
    water *[1 mark]*
10. The solution will change from red to yellow *[1 mark]*
11. $Cu \rightarrow Cu^{2+} + 2e^-$ *[1 mark]*
12. E.g. filter out the precipitate from the solution using filter paper and a filter funnel *[1 mark]*. Rinse the precipitate and filter paper with deionised water *[1 mark]*. Leave the calcium sulfate to dry in an oven/desiccator *[1 mark]*.

Answers

Test 8: Extracting Metals and Equilibria
Pages 16–17

1. B [1 mark] 2. B [1 mark]
3. A [1 mark] 4. A [1 mark]
5. A [1 mark] 6. C [1 mark]
7. C [1 mark] 8. B [1 mark]
9. Metal: Any metal that's above carbon in the reactivity series, e.g. aluminium [1 mark].
Explanation: It's extracted by electrolysis because it's too reactive to be extracted by reduction with carbon/it is above carbon in the reactivity series [1 mark].
10. The reaction of magnesium with hydrochloric acid would produce a lot of bubbles/effervescence [1 mark]. The reaction of iron with hydrochloric acid would be less vigorous/produce fewer bubbles than with magnesium [1 mark]. Magnesium reacts faster than iron because magnesium is more reactive/higher in the reactivity series than iron [1 mark].
11. E.g. nitrogen gas (N_2) can be obtained from the air [1 mark]. Hydrogen gas (H_2) can be produced from natural gas [1 mark].

Test 9: Extracting Metals and Equilibria
Pages 18–19

1. A [1 mark] 2. C [1 mark]
3. C [1 mark] 4. B [1 mark]
5. A [1 mark] 6. A [1 mark]
7. C [1 mark] 8. A [1 mark]
9. E.g. getting the raw materials [1 mark], manufacturing the product [1 mark], using the product [1 mark], disposal of the product [1 mark].
10. Any two from: e.g. recycling doesn't require new ore to be mined, which would damage the landscape/destroy habitats. / Recycling is likely to reduce the amount of metal which takes up space in landfill and can pollute the surroundings. / Recycling generally uses less energy than extracting from ores, and the energy used to extract from ores is often produced by burning fossil fuels. [2 marks]
11. Metal A is more reactive than metal B [1 mark].

Test 10: Separate Chemistry 1
Pages 20–21

1. A [1 mark] 2. A [1 mark]
3. B [1 mark] 4. B [1 mark]
5. C [1 mark] 6. C [1 mark]
7. B [1 mark] 8. A [1 mark]
9. There are fewer molecules of gas products than gas reactants [1 mark], so increasing the pressure favours the forward reaction, meaning a higher yield [1 mark]. Increased pressure also increases the rate of reaction, so equilibrium is reached faster [1 mark].
10. Convert 25.0 cm³ and 40.0 cm³ to dm³:
Volume of KOH = 25.0 ÷ 1000 = 0.0250 dm³
Volume of H_2SO_4 = 40.0 ÷ 1000 = 0.0400 dm³ [1 mark]
Number of moles of KOH = concentration × volume = 0.200 × 0.0250 [1 mark] = 0.00500 mol
From the equation, 2 moles of KOH reacts with 1 mole of H_2SO_4, so there were 0.00500 ÷ 2 = 0.00250 moles of H_2SO_4 in the acid solution [1 mark].
So acid concentration = moles ÷ volume = 0.00250 ÷ 0.0400 = 0.0625 mol dm^{-3} [1 mark]
[Or 4 marks for the correct answer via any other method.]

Test 11: Separate Chemistry 1
Pages 22–23

1. B [1 mark] 2. B [1 mark]
3. C [1 mark] 4. B [1 mark]
5. A [1 mark] 6. C [1 mark]
7. A [1 mark] 8. B [1 mark]
9. Atom economy = (total M_r of desired products ÷ total M_r of all products) × 100
$= \frac{(24 + (35.5 \times 2))}{(24 + (35.5 \times 2)) + (2 \times 1)} \times 100$
$= \frac{95}{97} \times 100$ [1 mark].
Atom economy = 97.9... = 98% (to 2 s.f.) [1 mark]
10. brass [1 mark]
E.g. brass is harder than either of the metals from which it is made. / Brass provides low amounts of friction [1 mark]
11. 2 moles of oxygen → 1 mole of carbon dioxide, therefore 2 volumes of oxygen → 1 volume of carbon dioxide. So the volume of carbon dioxide formed = 120 ÷ 2 = 60 dm³ [1 mark].
1 mole of gas = 24 dm³, so 60 dm³ = 60 ÷ 24 = 2.5 moles of gas [1 mark].
Mass of CO_2 = moles × M_r = 2.5 × 44 = 110 g [1 mark].
[Or 3 marks for the correct answer via any other method.]

Mixed Tests for Paper 1
Test 12: Paper 1 Mixed Topics
Pages 24–25

1. B [1 mark] 2. C [1 mark]
3. C [1 mark] 4. B [1 mark]
5. A [1 mark] 6. A [1 mark]
7. C [1 mark] 8. B [1 mark]
9. Strong acids are acids that ionise almost completely in water [1 mark].
10. Any two from: e.g. high melting point / high density / formation of coloured compounds / catalytic activity [2 marks]
11. E.g. industrial production of ammonium sulfate does not use burettes/steam baths/crystallisation [1 mark], because they are not suitable for the large quantities, required in industry [1 mark]. Industrial production has more stages than laboratory preparation [1 mark], because the ammonia and sulfuric acid have to be made from their raw materials first [1 mark].

Test 13: Paper 1 Mixed Topics
Pages 26–27

1. A [1 mark] 2. A [1 mark]
3. B [1 mark] 4. C [1 mark]
5. A [1 mark] 6. C [1 mark]
7. A [1 mark] 8. A [1 mark]
9. E.g. they produce no pollutants [1 mark]. They are more energy-efficient [1 mark].
10. The forwards reaction would be favoured. The right hand side of the equation contains fewer molecules of gas [1 mark], so the equilibrium would move towards the right/products to reduce the pressure [1 mark].
11. Copper [1 mark]
Copper is less reactive than hydrogen, so it will be produced at the cathode (instead of hydrogen gas) [1 mark].
12. The salt is soluble, so would be contaminated by the excess alkali [1 mark].

Test 14: Paper 1 Mixed Topics
Pages 28–29

1. B [1 mark] 2. A [1 mark]
3. C [1 mark] 4. C [1 mark]
5. C [1 mark] 6. A [1 mark]
7. B [1 mark] 8. B [1 mark]
9. Potassium, because it is more reactive/higher in the reactivity series than copper [1 mark], so it loses electrons more easily [1 mark].

Answers

10. M_r of NaOH = 23 + 16 + 1 = 40 *[1 mark]*
    concentration in g dm^{-3} = concentration in mol dm^{-3} × M_r
    = 0.5 × 40 = 20 g dm^{-3} *[1 mark]*
    [Or 2 marks for the correct answer via any other method.]

11. E.g. add water to the mixture to dissolve the soluble magnesium sulfate *[1 mark]*. Filter the mixture to remove the insoluble copper filings *[1 mark]*. Crystallise the remaining solution to obtain a pure sample of the magnesium sulfate *[1 mark]*.

Test 15: Paper 1 Mixed Topics
Pages 30–31

1. B *[1 mark]*
2. B *[1 mark]*
3. B *[1 mark]*
4. C *[1 mark]*
5. A *[1 mark]*
6. C *[1 mark]*
7. A *[1 mark]*
8. A *[1 mark]*
9. Relative atomic mass = [sum of (relative isotopic mass × isotopic abundance)] ÷ (sum of abundances)
    $= \dfrac{((63 \times 69.2) + (6.5 \times 30.8))}{(69.2 + 30.8)}$ *[1 mark]*
    = 63.616
    = 63.6 (to 3 s.f.) *[1 mark]*
    [Or 2 marks for the correct answer via any other method]
10. Metals that are low in the reactivity series are below carbon, so they can be extracted by carbon reduction *[1 mark]*. Metals that are high/above carbon in the reactivity series have to be extracted by electrolysis *[1 mark]*. Carbon reduction is less expensive than electrolysis because it requires a lot less energy *[1 mark]*.
11. Percentage yield = (actual yield ÷ theoretical yield) ×100
    = (59 ÷ 81) × 100 *[1 mark]*
    = 72.8...% ≈ 73% (to 2 s.f.) *[1 mark]*
    [Or 2 marks for the correct answer via any other method]

Test 16: Paper 1 Mixed Topics
Pages 32–33

1. C *[1 mark]*
2. A *[1 mark]*
3. A *[1 mark]*
4. B *[1 mark]*
5. C *[1 mark]*
6. C *[1 mark]*
7. A *[1 mark]*
8. B *[1 mark]*
9. The breaking down of a substance/electrolyte using electricity *[1 mark]*.
10. The forward and backward reactions are occurring at exactly the same rate *[1 mark]*.
11. Group 4 *[1 mark]*, as it has four electrons in its outer shell *[1 mark]*.

12. Increasing the temperature means the reaction takes place much quicker / at a faster rate *[1 mark]* but the yield is reduced *[1 mark]*. 450 °C is a compromise between maximum reaction rate and yield *[1 mark]*.

Topics for Paper 2

Test 17: Groups in the Periodic Table
Pages 34–35

1. B *[1 mark]*
2. C *[1 mark]*
3. B *[1 mark]*
4. C *[1 mark]*
5. A *[1 mark]*
6. C *[1 mark]*
7. B *[1 mark]*
8. C *[1 mark]*
9. A displacement reaction will occur if the halogen is more reactive than the halogen in the halide salt *[1 mark]*.
10. As you move down the group, the outer electron is further away from the nucleus *[1 mark]*. So it is less strongly attracted to the nucleus and is lost more easily *[1 mark]*.
11. The noble gases have a full outer shell of electrons *[1 mark]*, so they don't easily lose or gain electrons *[1 mark]*.
12. $Cl_{2(g)} + 2Na_{(s)} \rightarrow 2NaCl_{(s)}$
    [1 mark for correctly balanced equation, 1 mark for correct state symbols]

Test 18: Groups in the Periodic Table
Pages 36–37

1. C *[1 mark]*
2. B *[1 mark]*
3. B *[1 mark]*
4. B *[1 mark]*
5. B *[1 mark]*
6. C *[1 mark]*
7. A *[1 mark]*
8. B *[1 mark]*
9. E.g. helium has a lower density than air *[1 mark]*, so a balloon filled with helium will float *[1 mark]*.
10. Reduced: Cl_2/chlorine *[1 mark]*
    Oxidised: Br^-/bromide ions *[1 mark]*
11. The halogens decrease in reactivity down the group *[1 mark]*. This is because atomic radius increases down the group / the outer shell of electrons is further from the nucleus *[1 mark]*, so it is harder to attract/gain an extra electron *[1 mark]*.

Test 19: Rates of Reaction and Energy Changes
Pages 38–39

1. A *[1 mark]*
2. C *[1 mark]*
3. A *[1 mark]*
4. A *[1 mark]*
5. B *[1 mark]*
6. C *[1 mark]*
7. B *[1 mark]*
8. B *[1 mark]*

9. E.g. Experiment 2 could have been carried out at a higher temperature / with a greater concentration of reactants / at a higher pressure (with gases) / with a catalyst / with solid reactants crushed into smaller parts *[1 mark]*. This would have increased the rate of reaction, as shown by the steeper gradient of the line *[1 mark]*.
10. E.g. carry out the reaction on a mass balance and record the decrease in mass *[1 mark]* and the time it takes for the reaction to finish *[1 mark]*. Calculate the average rate of reaction by dividing the decrease in mass by the time taken *[1 mark]*. / Using a gas syringe, record the volume of gas given off *[1 mark]* and the time it takes for the reaction to finish *[1 mark]*. Calculate the average rate of reaction by dividing the volume of gas by the time taken *[1 mark]*.
11. It shows an exothermic reaction. The products are at a lower energy than the reactants *[1 mark]*, so energy is released and the reaction must be exothermic *[1 mark]*.

Test 20: Rates of Reaction and Energy Changes
Pages 40–41

1. B *[1 mark]*
2. B *[1 mark]*
3. B *[1 mark]*
4. B *[1 mark]*
5. A *[1 mark]*
6. C *[1 mark]*
7. A *[1 mark]*
8. B *[1 mark]*
9. Increasing the concentration of a solution increases the number of reactant particles in a given volume/causes the particles to move closer together *[1 mark]* so will increase the frequency of collisions/cause the particles to collide more often *[1 mark]*.
10. Find the energy required to break the bonds:
    4(C–H) + 2(O=O)
    = (4 × 413) + (2 × 496)
    = 2644 kJ mol^{-1} *[1 mark]*
    Find the energy released when forming new bonds:
    2(C=O) + 4(O–H)
    = (2 × 803) + (4 × 464)
    = 3462 kJ mol^{-1} *[1 mark]*
    So the energy change
    = 2644 – 3462 *[1 mark]*
    = –818 kJ mol^{-1} *[1 mark]*
    [Or 4 marks for the correct answer via any other method.]
11. The yeast produces enzymes which serve as a catalyst for the fermentation reaction *[1 mark]*.

Answers

Test 21: Fuels and Earth Science
Pages 42–43
1. B *[1 mark]* 2. C *[1 mark]*
3. C *[1 mark]* 4. A *[1 mark]*
5. C *[1 mark]* 6. B *[1 mark]*
7. C *[1 mark]* 8. A *[1 mark]*
9. Carbon dioxide *[1 mark]*.
E.g. methane / ammonia / water vapour (steam) / nitrogen *[1 mark]*.
From volcanic activity *[1 mark]*.
10. Decane has the lower viscosity, because decane molecules are shorter than icosane molecules *[1 mark]*. This means there are weaker intermolecular forces holding the molecules together and therefore the liquid can flow more easily *[1 mark]*.
11. Any one from: e.g. burning fossil fuels, as combustion of hydrocarbons in the fuels produces carbon dioxide. / Deforestation, as this reduces the number of trees which can remove carbon dioxide from the air. *[1 mark for a correct activity, 1 mark for a correct explanation]*

Test 22: Fuels and Earth Science
Pages 44–45
1. A *[1 mark]* 2. B *[1 mark]*
3. A *[1 mark]* 4. C *[1 mark]*
5. A *[1 mark]* 6. B *[1 mark]*
7. A *[1 mark]* 8. A *[1 mark]*
9. There is a temperature gradient in the column/the column gets cooler as you go up it *[1 mark]*. The fractions have different boiling points *[1 mark]* so they condense and drain out at different levels *[1 mark]*.
10. Advantage: e.g. the only waste product from hydrogen is water so hydrogen fuels cells don't produce pollutants. / Hydrogen can be obtained from water so it is a renewable resource. *[1 mark]*
Disadvantage: e.g. a hydrogen-powered car needs a special, expensive engine. / A lot of energy is needed to extract hydrogen. / Hydrogen is hard to store. / Hydrogen is not widely available. *[1 mark]*
11. Green plants decreased the carbon dioxide level and increased the oxygen level *[1 mark]*. The process that caused this change is photosynthesis *[1 mark]*.

Test 23: Separate Chemistry 2
Pages 46–47
1. B *[1 mark]* 2. B *[1 mark]*
3. A *[1 mark]* 4. C *[1 mark]*
5. B *[1 mark]* 6. B *[1 mark]*
7. A *[1 mark]* 8. B *[1 mark]*
9. Any two from: e.g. instrumental analysis is much faster / more sensitive / more accurate than chemical tests *[1 mark each]*.
10. Iron(II) / Fe^{2+} *[1 mark]*
Bromide / Br^- *[1 mark]*
11. They contain fewer hydrogen atoms than the alkane with the same number of carbon atoms / a carbon-carbon double bond *[1 mark]*.
12. E.g. drugs, because the small size of nanoparticles means they can be absorbed easily by the body. / Electronic circuits, because nanoparticles such as carbon nanotubes conduct electricity. / Catalysts, because nanoparticles have a very high surface area to volume ratio. *[1 mark for a valid use, 1 mark for a correct explanation]*

Test 24: Separate Chemistry 2
Pages 48–49
1. B *[1 mark]* 2. B *[1 mark]*
3. B *[1 mark]* 4. C *[1 mark]*
5. B *[1 mark]* 6. C *[1 mark]*
7. B *[1 mark]* 8. A *[1 mark]*
9. Add sodium hydroxide to both solutions until it is in excess *[1 mark]*. The precipitate formed with the aluminium chloride solution will redissolve but the precipitate formed with the calcium chloride will remain *[1 mark]*.
10.
$$\begin{array}{c} H \\ \diagdown \\ \end{array} C = C \begin{array}{c} F \\ \diagup \\ \end{array}$$
$$\begin{array}{c} \diagup \\ H \\ \end{array} \qquad \begin{array}{c} \diagdown \\ F \\ \end{array}$$ *[1 mark]*
11. Recycling:
Advantage — e.g. produces less emissions than burning / uses less resources than making new plastic / creates jobs *[1 mark]*
Disadvantage — e.g. it is difficult/ expensive to separate different polymer types / recycled polymers may be lower quality than new polymers *[1 mark]*
Combustion:
Advantage — e.g. produces energy which can be used to generate electricity *[1 mark]*
Disadvantage — e.g. can release toxic gases / can release carbon dioxide, which contributes to global warming *[1 mark]*

Test 25: Separate Chemistry 2
Pages 50–51
1. C *[1 mark]* 2. C *[1 mark]*
3. C *[1 mark]* 4. C *[1 mark]*
5. B *[1 mark]* 6. A *[1 mark]*
7. A *[1 mark]* 8. B *[1 mark]*
9. Addition polymerisation *[1 mark]*. Ethene molecules have C=C double bonds which can open up and join together to form a chain *[1 mark]*.
10. E.g. B would be unsuitable because it has low corrosion resistance *[1 mark]*. A is more suitable than C because A is stronger and more corrosion resistant *[1 mark]*. A is more expensive, but as surgical instruments are fairly small, this is a less significant factor *[1 mark]*.
11. A carboxylic acid will form *[1 mark]* because this molecule has an -OH functional group, so it is an alcohol and will react in the same way as other alcohols *[1 mark]*.

Mixed Tests for Paper 2

Test 26: Paper 2 Mixed Topics
Pages 52–53
1. C *[1 mark]* 2. B *[1 mark]*
3. B *[1 mark]* 4. A *[1 mark]*
5. A *[1 mark]* 6. B *[1 mark]*
7. B *[1 mark]* 8. C *[1 mark]*
9. E.g. they could build up in cells / cause lung inflammation if breathed in *[1 mark]*.
10. Decane will have a higher boiling point because it has a longer hydrocarbon chain/is a bigger molecule *[1 mark]* and therefore has stronger intermolecular forces *[1 mark]*.
11. Divide the reacting mass of calcium by its A_r and divide the reacting mass of oxygen gas by its M_r to give the number of moles:
Ca: 200 ÷ 40 = 5 moles *[1 mark]*
O_2: 80 ÷ 32 = 2.5 moles *[1 mark]*
So 5 moles of Ca reacts with 2.5 moles of O_2. This simplifies to 2:1 *[1 mark]*.
Since calcium forms Ca^{2+} ions and oxygen forms O^{2-} ions, the formula for calcium oxide is CaO.
So the symbol equation is
$2Ca + O_2 \rightarrow 2CaO$ *[1 mark]*.
[Or 4 marks for the correct answer via any other method.]

Answers

Test 27: Paper 2 Mixed Topics
Pages 54–55
1. C *[1 mark]* 2. B *[1 mark]*
3. A *[1 mark]* 4. B *[1 mark]*
5. A *[1 mark]* 6. B *[1 mark]*
7. A *[1 mark]* 8. A *[1 mark]*
9. Find the number of moles in 1.84 g of ethanol: moles = mass ÷ M_r
   = 1.84 ÷ 46 = 0.04 moles *[1 mark]*
   1 mole of ethanol reacts to form 2 moles of carbon dioxide, so 0.04 moles of ethanol reacts to form
   0.04 × 2 = 0.08 moles of carbon dioxide *[1 mark]*
   [Or 2 marks for the correct answer via any other method.]
10. Each carbon atom only forms three covalent bonds *[1 mark]*, so each carbon atom has one electron that is delocalised *[1 mark]*. The delocalised electrons can move and conduct electricity *[1 mark]*.
11. The amount of time taken for the black cross to disappear will decrease *[1 mark]* because increasing the temperature increases the rate of the reaction *[1 mark]*.

Test 28: Paper 2 Mixed Topics
Pages 56–57
1. A *[1 mark]* 2. A *[1 mark]*
3. A *[1 mark]* 4. C *[1 mark]*
5. A *[1 mark]* 6. A *[1 mark]*
7. A *[1 mark]* 8. B *[1 mark]*
9. It will increase the rate of the reaction *[1 mark]* because the surface area to volume ratio of the solid is increased *[1 mark]*, meaning collisions can occur more frequently between reactants *[1 mark]*.
10. Pentanol *[1 mark]*
11. Moles = mass ÷ M_r
    moles (copper) = 25.4 ÷ 63.5 = 0.4
    moles (chlorine) = 28.4 ÷ 35.5 = 0.8
    [1 mark]
    Ratio of Cu : Cl is 1 : 2 *[1 mark]*
    So empirical formula = $CuCl_2$ *[1 mark]*

Test 29: Paper 2 Mixed Topics
Pages 58–59
1. B *[1 mark]* 2. A *[1 mark]*
3. B *[1 mark]* 4. A *[1 mark]*
5. C *[1 mark]* 6. A *[1 mark]*
7. C *[1 mark]* 8. B *[1 mark]*
9. Chlorine has more than one isotope *[1 mark]*. Relative atomic mass is an average that takes into account the relative abundances of all the isotopes of an element *[1 mark]*.
10. So you know exactly which ions are in a sample / there can be no confusion about the identity of an ion *[1 mark]*
11. E.g. they are very stiff/hard, so will withstand weight / keep their shape *[1 mark]*.
12.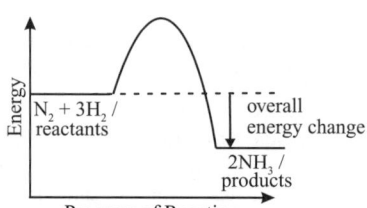

[1 mark for labelled product line below and to the right of labelled reactant line, 1 mark for correct shape of curve linking reactants to products, 1 mark for correct labelling of overall energy change]

Test 30: Paper 2 Mixed Topics
Pages 60–61
1. B *[1 mark]* 2. B *[1 mark]*
3. C *[1 mark]* 4. C *[1 mark]*
5. B *[1 mark]* 6. A *[1 mark]*
7. A *[1 mark]* 8. B *[1 mark]*
9. The Earth radiates long wavelength (infrared) radiation *[1 mark]*, which is absorbed by greenhouse gases in the atmosphere *[1 mark]*. The greenhouse gases re-emit some of the radiation back to Earth *[1 mark]*. The radiation is heat radiation so this results in the warming of the Earth *[1 mark]*.
10. butanoic acid *[1 mark]*
11. Line 2, because it has a lower initial rise in energy than line 1 *[1 mark]*, which shows the activation energy has been lowered by a catalyst *[1 mark]*.